DEMONSTRATION OF THE FAITH

Theodore Abu Qurrah
Bishop of Harran

Translated by: D.P. Curtin

Copyright @ 2021 Dalcassian Press

All rights reserved. No part of this publication may be reproduced, distributed, or transmitted in any form or by any means, including photocopying, recording, or other electronic or mechanical methods, without the prior written permission of the publisher, except in the case of brief quotations embodied in critical reviews and certain other non-commercial uses permitted by copyright law. For permission request, write to Dalcassian Press at dalcassianpublishing at gmail.com

ISBN: 979-8-3302-3447-9 (Paperback)

Library of Congress Control Number:
Author: Curtin, D.P. (1985-)

Printed by Ingram Content Group, 1 Ingram Blvd, La Vergne, Tennessee

First printing edition 2021.

DEMONSTRATION OF THE FAITH

Demonstration of the Faith of the Church by the Two Testaments and the Councils

Theodore Abu Qurrah
Translated into French by: Constantin Bacha

Demonstration of the Holy Law of Moses and the Prophets who announced the Messiah. Of the holy Gospel preached to the Gentiles by the Apostles of Christ born of the Virgin Mary. Of the orthodoxy attributed by all men to the Chalcedonians. and Refutation of the doctrines of all the sects which call themselves Christian by the magister-philosopher, our saint Father Theodore, bishop of Haran.

God appeared to Moses at Mount Sinai and chose him to be the lawgiver of the children of Israel. He ordered him to go to Pharaoh, king of Egypt, to deliver the children of Israel out of his hands. Moses, frightened by the magnitude of the task that the Lord wanted to entrust to him, excused himself from this mission by apologizing thus: "Who am I to go to Pharaoh and deliver your people from his hand?" The Lord said to him. : "I will help you and uphold you in your words; therefore go and summon the heads of the children of Israel and say to them: 'The Lord God of your fathers, the God of Abraham, the God of Isaac, the God of Jacob, has sent me for you." Moses said to the Lord: "If I go to the children of Israel and say to them: 'The God of your fathers has sent me for you, what will they say if they ask what is his name? "The Lord said to Moses: "You will answer them: "He who does not cease to be has sent me to you." be; I am the God of Abraham, the God of Isaac, the God of Jacob." Moses replied thus: "Suppose I go and say these words to them, what will they say if they say to me: 'You are a liar, the Lord has not appeared to you? "The Lord said to Moses: "What do you have in your hand?" Moses answered him: "A rod." The Lord said to Moses, "Throw her to the ground." Moses threw it away, and it was changed into a serpent, which frightened Moses so that he fled. The Lord said again to Moses: "Take him by the tail." Moses grabbed the serpent by the tail and it turned into a rod again. The Lord added: "Put your hand under your sleeve." Moses did so, and instantly his hand was covered with leprosy as white as snow. The Lord said to him again: "Put your hand back under your sleeve." Moses put it back and he took it out again with the same color of his flesh. The Lord also said to Moses: "If the children of Israel believe in the first miracle, you will have achieved your goal; if they do not believe, they will believe in the second; and if they do not even believe in the second, take water of the Nile and pour it on the earth; it will be turned into blood, to let them know that the God of their fathers has sent you. So when Moses received the gift of miracles from God, he reluctantly agreed to go to Egypt. We must conclude, from the above, that the reasonable and attentive man must not accept anyone's religion without miracles: for Moses knew well that if he claimed to be elected by God as legislator, without proving his mission by the miracles that only God can work in his favor, any man could deny and despise him by casting him out; and if he were equipped with the gift of miracles, he would have weapons strong enough to convince anyone who sincerely wants his salvation and lead them to embrace the religion he preaches to them. Therefore, the reasonable man must not accept a religion not founded on divine miracles which prove that its legislator is from God; he who therefore embraces a religion without this condition, neglects the most important matter for which God gave intelligence to man and he risks losing himself by letting himself be led to his ruin by someone who wants to remove him from religion. path of truth which leads to the blessed life after which spirits aspire. Those therefore who accepted the religion preached by Moses are on the right path; because he proved the divinity of his mission by working the miracles which can only be done by the omnipotence of God. So, when Moses spoke to them of things past, how God created heaven and earth, and told them things which they did not know, they did well to believe in him; for God only grants the gift of miracles to those who do his will and work for the conversion of others. Thus, Jesus Christ our God, true Wisdom, began to preach his Gospel only after having proven his divine Omnipotence by miracles; allowing all who were afflicted by infirmities and diseases to come to him to heal them. Crowds then flocked to him from Galilee, from Jerusalem, and from the countries beyond the Jordan. When he saw himself surrounded by these crowds, he called his Apostles and began the preaching of his doctrine, saying: "Blessed are the poor in spirit, for they have the kingdom of heaven." And he continued the promulgation of his law thereafter, always accompanying his precepts with miracles, like Moses, until he had accomplished the entire economy of his life by dying on the cross, being buried and resurrected. the third day. Therefore, those who received Jesus Christ because of his countless miracles are also on the right track and they also have much stronger motives than those who received Moses for his miracles. If you draw a parallel between the two, you undoubtedly find Jesus much superior to Moses, although he too is great, because the miracles of Jesus are innumerable. He did not limit himself to the miracles that he performed himself, but he granted his Apostles the power to perform them in his name. Moses performed miracles, but few in number, and by the Almighty Power of God, his order and his help, not by his own strength; nevertheless, he said to no one: "Go and do miracles in my name." It was right that he should have been so of the two. Because Jesus Christ is God and Son of God, therefore he is able to work miracles by his own virtue and to grant this power to whomever he pleases to do similar miracles in his name. But Moses was only a servant and he did not work miracles by his own strength, but by the Almighty Power of God; this is why he did not do any before receiving the express order from God or resorting to prayer to ask God to grant him to do so. Moses performed miracles by the Almighty Power of God and his command or by resorting to his help; in the same way the Apostles performed miracles not in the name of God, but of Jesus Christ, by his strength and his order or by resorting to his help. Furthermore, the Apostles were much superior to Moses: for the latter only performed his miracles after having received the order from God or after having resorted to his assistance through prayer; but the Apostles often performed their miracles without praying; they only said: "In the name of Jesus Christ, may this dead man rise, may this blind man open his eyes, may this paralytic be healed!" and the effect always responded immediately to their words. They did not limit themselves there; for Saint Peter, passing among the sick, healed those who found themselves in his very shadow; the mantle of Saint Paul also healed the sick on whom it was imposed. David's word was therefore fulfilled in the Apostles, when he said: "God gives great power to the word of those who bring good news." (Ps. Lxvii, 12.) The Jews had less reason to welcome Moses than the Gentiles had to accept Jesus Christ; for the latter surpasses Moses as much as the light of the sun surpasses in brightness that of the lamp. The Gentiles could be content with the miracles that the Apostles performed in their presence in the name of their Master: these miracles alone must make them welcome Jesus Christ and believe in all that he said about himself and in all that his Apostles reported about him, without resorting to the preaching of Moses and other prophets in his favor. When Moses presented himself to the children of Israel, they, in fact, believed in his mission and accepted everything he brought them from God, for the sole miracles he performed in their presence, although no previous prophet predicted its coming. The children of Israel did not require from him, in addition to these miracles, the prophecy of another prophet in his favor to prove his mission. Likewise the Gentiles could rightly believe in Jesus Christ because of his innumerable miracles and those of his Apostles without recourse to the previous preaching of Moses and other prophets in his favor. Therefore, with even greater reason, we must welcome Jesus Christ with more eagerness than those who received Moses, because of the advantage of being predicted by Moses and all the other prophets who announced his coming and all the economy of his life; like his crucifixion (Is.,lxv, 2), his pierced side (Zac, XII, 10), his hands and feet nailed, his garment cast by lot (Ps. xxi, 18), his face stained with spittle (Es ., l, 6), his back covered with blows (Ps. lxxii, 14), his wounds atoning for the sins of men and healing the weaknesses of their faults (Is., him, 5), the vinegar he took with the gall of bitterness. (Ps. Lxviii, 22.) All these passages are well known in the books of the prophets, and they are very precise. I am surprised, Jew, that you received Moses because of his few miracles, and that you refuse to receive Jesus Christ with his innumerable miracles. If you are righteous, you should have accepted him without the preachings of Moses and other prophets, just as you accepted Moses for his miracles alone without asking him for a previous prophecy to prove his mission. If Moses had forbidden you to accept the prophets who were to come after him, as Jesus Christ did to his disciples, you would be right to doubt Jesus Christ; but on the contrary, Moses, in his holy law, promised you a prophet who should come after him and he orders you in a very precise way to listen to him and obey him in everything he commands you. He still threatens you with death if you refuse to listen to him. He also says in a more precise way that this prophet is, like him, a legislator and master of a new alliance. (Deut. xviii, 15-18.) This specific prophecy obliges you to receive this unique prophet whom Moses orders you to obey without taking into account all the other prophets. And when Moses told you the prophecy of Jacob which said: "The prophecy will never disappear from you until the coming of the Messiah who is the hope of the nations" (Gen., Lxix, 10), he justified and approved in general all the prophets who were before Jesus Christ; and in particular this one prophet whom he has often commanded you, on behalf of God, to obey. So the preaching of the coming of this prophet-legislator by Moses does not let you hesitate for a moment to welcome Jesus - Christ and to believe in him because of these miracles that he has done. You must reason like this: "The prophet whom Moses ordered me to obey is undoubtedly this Jesus who performed innumerable miracles, as many as Moses ever did; and if Moses had said nothing about him, these miracles alone oblige me with reason to accept him without requiring previous preaching in his favor to prove his mission in the same way as I accepted Moses." You must know, Jew, that this prophet is legislator and master of a new covenant; This is why the Lord has ordered you in a very particular way to obey him, and he has often reiterated this order to you. This is what he says in Jeremiah: "The days are coming, says the Lord, when I will make a new covenant for the children of Israel and for the house of Judah, not as I made for their fathers when I brought them out of the land of Egypt." (Jer., xxxi, 31.) David said to the Lord: "Give them, Lord, a lawgiver, that the nations may know that they are men." (Ps. ix, 20.) You say, Jew: "My ancestors, who were contemporaries of this Jesus and who saw him, are all dead, and therefore I do not know that he worked miracles." We will say to you: It is very easy for you to know this, if you sincerely desire your salvation; for you should have known that Jesus Christ performed these miracles which converted the Gentiles, and made them embrace his doctrine by making war against their minds, their passions and their pleasures, so that they left the abundance for poverty, license for chastity, wealth for the anxieties of life, weakness for mortifications, and pleasures for complete renunciation of the world, the pleasures of the flesh and honors. He forces them to suffer death, and all kinds of torture, rather than deny him; He said to them, "Whoever denies me before men, him will I deny before my Father who is in heaven." He also said to them:

"What I tell you in secret, declare from the housetops. Do not fear that which takes away the life of the body and cannot take away the life of the soul; but fear him who can take away the life of the body and that of the soul and throw both into the fire of hell. He also says: "He who loses his soul for me will find it in eternal life." He also said: "Whoever follows me and does not hate his father, his mother, his brothers, his sisters, his children and all his relatives for my sake is not worthy of me." He said to them: "I leave you like sheep among wolves." Elsewhere he said to them: "The world will rejoice and you will be sad." (Joan, xvi, 20.) "The days are coming when whoever kills you will think he is offering a sacrifice to God." (Joan., XVI, 2.) He forced them to mortify themselves by the deprivation of pleasures and the extermination of the least passion, saying: "Whoever strikes you on the cheek, present the other to him. Whoever wants you tear off your tunic, give him your coat again. If you look at a woman to lust after her, you have committed adultery in your heart. If you call your friend Raca or crazy, you deserve the fire of hell. He also said: "You have heard it said to the ancients: You shall love your friend and hate your enemy. And I say to you: Love your enemies and pray for them." Tell me, Jew, how the Gentiles were able to receive Jesus Christ with such a severe law which leads them to sacrifice themselves, with the weakness that he wanted to show by suffering the crucifixion with its pains and its reproaches. His enemies insulted him, they nailed his hands and feet while hanging him on the cross; they made him drink vinegar and take gall; they made him suffer so much that he let sweat flow from his body as strong as lumps of blood, and, being on the cross, he cried out: "My God, my God, why have you abandoned? "All this should have frightened those who heard it, and prevented them from following Jesus Christ and taking him for God as the Gentiles had done; for it is quite obvious that if these miracles recounted in the Gospels and the books of the Apostles had not really been performed, Jesus Christ would not have been received, because it was the miracles which constrained the spirits and obliged them to accept him. receive and believe in him. If Jesus Christ wanted to deceive (the world), he should have forbidden his Apostles from revealing these weaknesses to the Gentiles, and he should have ordered them to exalt him and make him greater and more beautiful than he was. ; he should have attracted them with a free and licentious doctrine to make their conversion quicker and easier. But he did none of this: he wanted to show himself thus dishonored to those to whom he preached his doctrine and he forced them to mortify themselves and die for his cause. It is very astonishing that Moses made God known and glorified him, reporting that he created heaven and earth, that he is higher than the sky, and that he exalted and praised him all manners; that he delivered the children of Israel from the tyranny of Pharaoh; that he separated for them the waters of the sea; that he made manna and quails fall from heaven; he made the waters flow from the rocks for them; he fought the nations for them; he promised them: "The Lord will help you to destroy the nations of Syria and possess their land," and 'he gave them a very broad law, nevertheless he could not convert any of the Gentiles. The children of Israel themselves did not believe well in his word or in his God because when the Lord came down; on Mount Sinai which he caused to tremble and smoke, the children of Israel were frightened by this aspect; but no sooner had they come down from Sinai than they worshiped the calf When the Apostles spread among the Gentiles. , they revealed to them the sufferings and the crucifixion of their Master with his words which indicate his weakness, and they obliged them to observe this very severe law which Jesus Christ gave; however everyone responded to their call. Who is unaware then that this happened by virtue of the miracles that the Apostles worked in the name of Jesus Christ in a way superior to those of Moses as heaven is to earth? You cannot say, Jew, that the Gentiles followed Jesus Christ out of partisanship, that is, out of zeal for the national religion they shared with him (nationalist). This reason is rather against you. We can rightly address this accusation to you, that you followed Moses who is of your people, out of party spirit of your national religion, with the hope of having a share in the honors and authority that God gave him. The same cannot be said of the Gentiles who followed Jesus Christ, because the Apostles who evangelized the Gentiles were Jews and they were preaching to them from a man believed to be Jewish. All this should have inspired them with aversion and horror towards him, because the Jews were, in general, the hated enemies of all nations; moreover, their doctrine had nothing of what one aspires to in this world, such as honors and power: it is completely opposed to that. Know well, Jew, that the Gentiles were only able to take Jesus Christ for God and submit to his law with this great and profound obedience which made them sacrifice their lives every day, by virtue of the miracles that the Apostles performed. in their presence in his name. You would say, Jew: The Gentiles followed Jesus Christ out of ignorance. If this be so, take these words which the Apostles spoke of Jesus Christ and take this law which he imposed upon them, and try to make one ignorant man believe or accept it. You will never be able to, because ignorant people hate these things more than anyone else. Like animals, they only seek to satisfy their pleasures; their intelligence is only capable of understanding vulgar and illusory speech. In truth, your religion has more attractions for these people than Christianity, because it greatly increases God and shows his terrible majesty; it allows licenses, it allows the enjoyment of honors, authority, honey and milk; it allows polygamy and divorce for the slightest reason, to subjugate the nations which will have to carry you on their shoulders, as you claim; they will be your slaves, and their daughters your servants; you will build a city of emerald and hyacinth. Such things can easily seduce ignorant minds and captivate their ambition, it is not surprising to have many supporters if you preach a religion so full of attractions, especially if it has been favored by a power which protects it. , as we have seen happen. You would say, Jew: Those who followed Jesus Christ were philosophers; it was philosophy that led them to him. You must therefore follow their example in this philosophy which led them to Jesus Christ, as you well admit. But these ignominious things which are reported of Jesus Christ, the philosophers or the wise men of this world do not believe them, they surpass all human intelligence; unless the Holy Spirit pours out his grace on their souls, teaching them by his light that Jesus Christ is God. Indeed, Saint Paul writes: "No one can say: Jesus Christ is God, except through the Holy Spirit." If you do not believe this, try to bring the Christian doctrine to all the philosophers of the world to make it accepted by only one; but I am sure that you never could, because the wise of this world only seek the honors of this world and believe only what is in conformity with the laws of nature which they study in a more particular way than the vulgar people: they boast of the subtlety of their speeches and the seductive harmony of expression. Christian doctrine is quite the opposite. Indeed, as Saint Paul says: "In the wisdom of God, the world did not know God through wisdom, and God loved to save those who believe in the foolishness of preaching." (I Cor., i, 21.) If you say, Jew: "These people were of average intelligence", you are not telling the truth; because people of average intelligence do nothing without reflection and resolution, and they only believe what is similar to the truths of which they have acquired certainty through sense and experience. Therefore, we cannot preach the Christian doctrine to those minds to whom it is repugnant and who reject it with contempt. Since you have accepted, Jew, what we have put forward, you must necessarily admit that the Gentiles only accepted Jesus Christ by the virtue of his miracles which they saw, according to the account of the Gospels and the books of the Apostles ; and by the grace of the Holy Spirit who enlightened their minds and convinced them that Jesus is God and Son of

God, something he said about himself. These Gentiles who accepted Jesus Christ number five-sixths in the world today. Although he suffered the passions and pains of the cross, he did not suffer all this in vain or out of weakness and impotence, but for very just reasons, hidden from souls that the Holy Spirit did not enlighten. by his grace. What we have said clearly proves that the Gentiles accepted Jesus Christ only by virtue of the miracles mentioned in the Gospels and the books of the Apostles. This necessarily compels your mind to believe and confess the truth of these miracles, as if you had seen them with your own eyes, for these are the miracles which have persuaded the Gentiles that Jesus Christ is truly God and the Son of God; now Jesus Christ and his Apostles testified that Moses and all the other prophets were messengers of God; therefore, by the testimony of Jesus Christ and that of his Apostles, Moses and the prophets are noted and proven as true messengers of God. If you are asked for a reason which proves (the divinity of) the mission of Moses or that of another prophet, you could not do it; for the law of Moses remained about five thousand years without being able to persuade any of the Gentiles that it was from God. Moreover, your fathers themselves did not preserve the law nor the true worship of God. But when Jesus Christ came, he persuaded all the Gentiles by his miracles, and he proved to them Moses and the other prophets, so that he became their preacher. He is right to do this and he must do it, for it is he who sent them with orders to announce them and characterize him, so that men would not reject him when they saw him walking on the earth. This is why Micah predicted his coming, saying: "Hear, all nations; be attentive, all people: let the Lord be witness against you; the Lord will go out from his place and come down to walk on the earth. for the sin of Jacob and because of the crimes of Israel." (Mich., i, 1-5.) Baruch had said of him: "He is our God, there is no other like him; he found the way of knowledge and gave it to Jacob his beloved and to Israel his friend. After this he appeared and walked among men. (Bar., iii, 36.) The Lord commanded Moses to make his brother Aaron priest and to offer sacrifices as he showed him in the mountain. (Ex., xxv, 40.) By these words he showed you that there is another priest of whom Aaron is the figure, and another sacrifice of which these sacrifices are the figure. David, who came in his time, explained to you that this priest of whom Aaron was the figure is the Lord who sits on the throne at the right hand of God and that he is the Son of God begotten of him before all ages: "The Lord said to my Lord: Sit at my right hand until I have put your enemies under your feet." (Ps. cix, 1.) God again said to his Son: "I have begotten you in my womb before the day." He said to him again: "You are the eternal Priest according to the order of Melchizedek." (Ps. cix, 1-4.) Isaiah, coming next, explained to you this sacrifice of which yours is the figure, reporting what the Messiah said about himself: "I do not disobey, I do not argue , I exposed my back to the whips and my cheek to the blows, and I did not turn my face from the affront of the spit." (Is., l, 6.) He says of him: "He is without appearance and without beauty; we have seen, he had neither appearance nor beauty: he had a miserable appearance more than all men; he is the wounded man who knows how to suffer illnesses; he was despised and without account; he bears our illnesses and he suffers for us; we thought he was wounded, struck by God; , it is because of our crimes that these afflictions happened to him, he took upon himself the chastisement of our salvation and we are healed by his wounds We are all lost, like sheep each of us has gone astray; and the Lord delivered him for our sins, when he was smitten he did not open his mouth; he was led as a sheep to the slaughter, and as a sheep sheared before him in silence; He didn't open his mouth." (Is., liii, 1-7.) All this shows you clearly, if you have intelligence, Jew, that your priest Aaron was the figure of this priest, and your sacrifice was the figure of this sacrifice; for if your priest atone for sins and your sacrifice atone for faults, the priest of whom David speaks would be useless, and in the same way this sacrifice of which Isaiah speaks would be established in vain by God, and Moses would be a liar in telling you that you have the face which David and Isaiah then explained. You did not then understand this as Moses said to you: "You have seen what God has done in your presence; but he has not given you eyes to see, nor ears to hear, nor understanding to understand. " (Deut., xix, 4.) If these things were not figures which symbolize realities, how could Moses tell you without lying; "You have seen what God did in your presence, but he has not given you eyes to see, nor ears to hear, nor understanding to understand? " This clearly indicates that you had the figures and symbols of the truth. David assures you by saying: "Our fathers did not understand your miracles in Egypt." (Ps. cv, 7.) This is sufficient to heal you, Jew, if you sincerely want the salvation of your soul like a reasonable man, and you would have been healed since then, if you accepted this from the holy Doctors of the Church that the Holy Spirit spoke and who explained everything concerning Jesus Christ through reason and the holy Books. Here then is a demonstration of Christian doctrine so well reasoned that it necessarily obliges every reasonable man of good will to accept it, because reason obviously leads to Jesus Christ, and he notes and justifies Moses and the Prophets; so we have the Old and the New Testament, and, as Solomon says in the Song of Songs: "On our gates are all the fruits, the old and the new." (vii, 13.) II But does this serve all Christians? It only serves us Chalcedonians; it is of no use to the Nestorians, nor to the Jacobites, nor to the Julianists (1), nor to the "Monothelites", nor to the other heretics who also call themselves Christians. Each of them takes for himself everything we have said to prove the divinity of Christianity, and he believes himself to be the true Christian. Having demonstrated Christianity and proven that it is the only, true among all other religions, we must separate our orthodox doctrine from all heresies, and prove that it is the only true and that all doctrines of these heresies are false. We have already proven it elsewhere, with the help of the Holy Spirit, in a delicate and precise study for intelligent people capable of studying obscure things that vulgar minds do not understand; but the precise and delicate study does not satisfy the common mind of the vulgar, the common people and the people of the fields and others, and does not in any way provide them with healing. We must therefore open up for them another clear and luminous path that can be followed surely and easily by people of superior intelligence and those of ordinary intelligence, that is to say the philosopher and the common people. This is why we are going to prove our orthodoxy and make its light shine as much as that of the sun whose rays are seen by young and old, so as not to leave anyone a pretext by abandoning it, to convince those who live peacefully in the the error of heresies, to rejoice the orthodox who, through the help of the Holy Spirit, are in the right faith and in the true religion, to excite them to unite justice and good works to this faith; it would not be useless to them but harmful, if they did not do what they must do in obedience to Christ. But what is this clear path that Orthodoxy shows us? We Christians together agree to accept and believe the books of the Old and New Testaments; but one thing separates us, our different interpretation of these books; this forces us to meet each in a separate church and prevents us from praying together in the same temple. This results in two things: that we are all equally pleasing to Christ by accepting the books of the Old and New Testaments dictated to us by the Holy Spirit and that God does not hold us accountable for not having penetrated the truths of these books, or that God does not accept to see us admit the letter of these books without the true meaning of the words that the Holy Spirit wanted to express in a way indispensable to religion. If someone says: Christ is content to see us follow these books without understanding their content, or the true meaning, he makes Christianity similar to Judaism, by putting the end of his doctrine in the words, not in the spirit; it allows Christians to come together to pray in a church at the same time as they are separated in spirit; he preaches to them to worship one God outwardly, and many gods inwardly; he persuades them to call themselves disciples of one Christ by mouth, while believing in many at the bottom of their hearts. But Christ does not want this worship, as he himself says: "I will never bring war in the place of peace." It is essential for every Christian, if he wants to be sincerely Christian, to adore Christ, the Father and the Holy Spirit in the proper sense of the books of the Old and New Testaments; otherwise he would be Jewish and could say, indifferently, that God is mutable or that there are several. When he hears Moses say: "God is a consuming fire" (Exod., xxiv, 17), he becomes a magician, because he conceives the fire which the wise men worship; and if he hears the prophet Daniel say: "He is the Ancient of days and his hair is white as pure wool" (Dan., seen, 9), he believes that God is very old; likewise, if he hears Ezekiel say: "It is from the middle of the body upwards all on fire like lapis lazuli, and from the middle downwards on fire" (Ezech., i, 27), he imagine that God has been changed from what he was, or that he is different from what Daniel saw and what Moses had already named. What a misfortune to see these three things disturbing the heart of the faithful! Moreover, if he hears Christ himself say that he is the door (Joan., x, 7), he believes him to be a material door, and if he hears him say that he is the vine (Joan., xv, 1), he thinks that he has been changed or that he is another different Christ, and so on. It is therefore necessary for him to follow the proper meaning of the book regarding the essence of religion, otherwise there would be no more worship. If this is so, the Church of Christ must necessarily be one of those churches each of which claims to have alone the true Christian doctrine. But what should common people, peasants, and all men in general, do who do not understand these truths which Christ commands them to believe in the way he wanted? Shall we say that he is asking the impossible of them? No; otherwise his descent from heaven and the shedding of his blood for them would be useless and even harmful to them: but as he does not require this of them, he does not ask the impossible of them, because we know well that, for the sake of Most, their intelligence cannot understand everything they need to know. How can we then find a path within the reach of their intelligence, so that by following it they all arrive at the possession of this truth? No heretic will ever know this path and be able to follow it; he possesses nothing of life except the word which he follows as in the darkness to deceive and seduce the simple; he chatters so that the simple, hearing him, believe that he is the source of wisdom; he wins them over to his party by uttering words unintelligible to them and even to him; as St. Paul says: "He does not understand what he says or what he reasons." (I Cor., XIX, 2.) Only the Orthodox possess this clear path, it leads them to eternal life; for we know well that Christ does not neglect this matter in condemning the majority of men to wander thus without being able to know a path which will lead their intelligence to understand what they must do. All the more so since Christ knew well, and the Apostles, that these heresies would exist and that Satan would use them to sift the Church so that it would keep the pure wheat. (Luke, xxii, 31.) The Holy Spirit clearly showed us this way through the mouth of Moses, the chief of the prophets, in the Pentateuch, when God gave him the rules according to which he was to govern the children of Israel. Moses gave these rules to their priests, who are the judges, and to whom he ordered to judge the children of Israel thus; he appointed leaders of ten, of fifty, of a hundred and of a thousand; He commanded them to carry out righteous judgment among the children of Israel, saying: "Look closely; what seems clear to you of these rules, use it with your brothers, and what seems obscure or doubtful to you, present it- me to take it to God and bring you the truth." (Deut, i, 10.) They did this all the time that Moses lived among them. When God permitted Moses to die beyond the Jordan, the prophet knew by the Holy Spirit that after his death the children of Israel would be in perplexity and doubt, therefore divided and scattered: therefore he gave them by the Holy Spirit a second law, leaving among them a successor who held his place forever: "If you find some obscure or doubtful commandments between blood and blood, between judgment and judgment, between impure and impure, and between quarrel and quarrel, and if there is a difference of opinion in your cities, come to the place which the Lord your God will choose to call on his name, and take refuge there and go and find the priests, the Levites and the judge who will exist. They will examine it and they will give you the right decision. Follow the decision that they give you in the place that the Lord your God will choose to call on his name and do what they command you. the law and the decision that they will give you; do not deviate from it either to the right or to the left. The man who through pride does not listen to the priest who acts in the name of the Lord, and to the judge who will be in these times, let him be put to death; strip the enemies of the children of Israel so that all the people may learn of this punishment and turn away from it, taking care not to imitate it." (Deut., xvii, 8.) You see clearly that Moses left no one, learned or not, the right to discuss these decisions But the Holy Spirit revealed to the prophet to entrust this authority to the college of priests and to the judge who will be in the place that God will choose to invoke his name there, leaving no one to discuss with them; but rather he ordered all the people, and everyone, learned or illiterate, to obey the decision issued by this college, for him or against him. He condemns to death the proud who does not want to accept their judgment with submission. , believing that his opinion is more just than theirs. He condemned to death anyone who does not accept their judgment because he was convinced that, the Holy Spirit having entrusted them to judge doubtful matters and disputes, he must assist their intelligence to tell the truth and does not abandon them without his help, whatever their condition and intelligence; he only lets them tell the truth. If someone said: "Although the Holy Spirit commands the people to obey the assembly of priests who will be in this place for obscure decisions, he allows them to say the false", he would consider that the Holy -Spirit himself deceives all the people, and he would be precisely a blasphemer against the Holy Spirit, by making the Holy Spirit, Sun of Justice and Source of Light, the cause of error. God forbid it be so! On the contrary, we are sure, and our hearts are at rest, that the Holy Spirit never abandons this assembly and does not allow it to pronounce any ill-timed judgment. In the new holy law of which the old was the figure, the Holy Spirit arranged things in the same way as in the old, by ordering any dispute between Christians, in matters of religion, to be brought to the assembly. of the Apostles and giving them a leader who ultimately judges all decisions with his assembly: to judge according to the views of the Holy Spirit, as shown in the Acts of the Apostles. When Paul and Barnabas were in Antioch, elected by the Holy Spirit to go through the cities and proclaim the Gospel of Christ, after they had accomplished the mission for which they were elected they returned to Antioch. Then there were brethren who came from Jerusalem to Antioch, teaching, and saying, "Unless you be circumcised according to the law of Moses, you cannot live." Paul and Barnabas opposed this; After a discussion, everyone decided that Paul and Barnabas, with some of them, would go up to see the Apostles and priests in Jerusalem about this dispute. When they arrived in Jerusalem, there were men of the party of the Pharisees who had embraced Christianity. They stood up and said to the Apostles: "The Gentiles who believe must be circumcised and commanded to keep the law of Moses." Then the Apostles met with the priests to study the dispute. A great discussion ensued. After this Peter stood up and said to them, "You know, my brothers, that the God of old wanted the Gentiles to hear the word of the gospel from me and to believe. God, who knows the hearts, justified them by giving them the Holy Spirit as well as us and he made no difference between them and us in purifying their hearts. Why then do you want to upset God and impose on the disciples a yoke that neither. neither we nor our fathers could bear? Yet we believe that we lived by the grace of our Lord Jesus as well as they." Then James answered, "Listen, men: Simon has told you how it pleased God to choose for himself a people from among the Gentiles. This agrees with the prophets, as it is written: 'After this I will come and rebuild the David's ruined dwelling; I will renew that which is demolished and I will make it rise again, that all men may seek the face of God with all the nations that are called by my name: this is what the Lord says who has done it. .'' Therefore I judge that those of the Gentiles who turn to God should not be troubled; but I see that they should be commanded to abstain from the filthiness of idols, from fornication, from the strangled flesh and some blood." Then all the Apostles and the priests with the whole Church judged and chose from among themselves two men, whom they sent to Antioch with Paul and Barnabas: the first is Jude surnamed Barsabas, and the other is Silas, the one and the another illustrious one among the brothers. They wrote (a letter) which they sent with them, and read thus: "To the Apostles, and to the Priests, and to the Brethren, to the Church which is at Antioch in Syria, and to the Brethren which are Gentiles, greetings. We have heard that some of us have gone from here to trouble you and have shaken your soul by telling you that you must be circumcised and keep the law of Moses, for which we did not command them. So we decided unanimously to choose two men and send them with our two brothers Barnabas and Paul who gave their lives for Christ. We appointed Jude and Silas to you and we ordered them to make you hear our word with their mouths. in these terms: It seemed good to the Holy Spirit and to us to impose no other obligation on you for what is necessary (for salvation), than to abstain from sacrifices, from idols, from blood, from the flesh choking and fornication. If you keep this, you are doing well." Jude and Silas bid farewell to the community and went down to Antioch where they gathered the faithful and gave them the letter, which they read with joy and consolation. Jude and Silas were prophets, they greatly comforted the brothers and strengthened them with many speeches. You see clearly: those who went to Antioch and commanded circumcision and keeping the law were from the community of the brethren of Jerusalem; Paul and Barnabas, who contradicted them, were also famous Apostles. When the two parties quarreled at Antioch, the Church did not accept (the opinion) of Paul and Barnabas nor that of the others; but she took them both to the assembly of the Apostles of which Saint Peter was the head. When the assembly of the Apostles had received them and had examined the dispute, they judged according to what they saw, attributing their judgment to the Holy Spirit and saying: "It seemed good to the Holy Spirit and to us." You see clearly that this assembly to which Christ has entrusted the right to judge heresies has no other view than that of the Holy Spirit. Any dispute in matters of doctrine must be brought to him; because no one, big or small, is allowed to have a different particular feeling, and no one has the right to impose his personal way of seeing on the Church. This is why the Church did not accept the opinion of Paul and Barnabas who were the light of the world, nor that of others. There is neither bishop nor patriarch nor any other person who can say to the Church: Receive what I say and reject what the Apostles say. It should be noted that the Apostles had as their leader Saint Peter to whom Christ had said: "You are Peter, and on this rock I will build my Church, and the gates of hell will not triumph over it" (Matt., XVI, 18); to whom he also said three times, after his resurrection, near the Sea of Tiberias: "Simon, do you love me? (If you love me) Feed my lambs, my rams and my sheep." (Joan., xxi, 15-18.) He said to him elsewhere: "Simon, Satan has asked to sift you as one sifts wheat, and I have prayed for you so that you do not lose your faith; but, at Now turn to your brothers and strengthen them." (Luke, XXII, 31.) You see clearly that Saint Peter is the foundation of the Church proper to the flock (of the faithful), and he who has his faith will never lose it; it is he also who is responsible for turning to his brothers and strengthening them. The words of the Lord: "I have prayed for you so that you do not lose your faith; but turn immediately to your brothers and strengthen them", do not designate the person of Peter nor the Apostles themselves- same. Christ wanted to designate with these words those who will hold the place of Saint Peter in Rome and the places of the Apostles. Likewise when he said to the Apostles: "I will be with you always until the end of the ages", he did not want to designate the persons of the Apostles alone, but also those who hold their places and all their flock. Thus by these words which he addressed to Saint Peter: "Turn immediately and strengthen your brothers, and let not your faith be lost", he wanted to designate his successors; for the reason that Saint Peter alone among the Apostles lost his faith and denied Christ, Christ had expressly abandoned him to show us that it was not his person that he wanted to designate, and we did not see no Apostle would fall so that Saint Peter would strengthen him. To say that Christ wanted to designate Saint Peter and the Apostles in person would be to deprive the

Church of what should strengthen it after the death of Saint Peter. How could this be? Seeing, after the death of the Apostles, Satan sifting through the Church, it is obvious that it is not them that Christ wanted to designate with these words. We all know, in fact, that it was after the death of the Apostles that the heresiarchs agitated the Church, namely: Paul of Samosata, Arius, Macedonius, Eunomius, Sabellius, Apollinarius, Origen and the others. If these words of the sacred text only designate the persons of Saint Peter and the Apostles, the Church would therefore have been deprived of consolation and would have had no one to save it from these heresiarchs and their doctrines which are the gates of hell which Christ said will never triumph over the Church. It is therefore quite obvious that these words designate the successors of Saint Peter, who in fact never cease to strengthen their brothers and will never cease until the end of the centuries. You know well that when Arius revolted, an assembly was assembled against him by the order of the bishop of Rome. The holy Council condemned him and put an end to his heresy; and the Church accepted the decision of this council and rejected Arius as the Church of Antioch had accepted the letter of the Apostles and had rejected those sectators who taught it circumcision and the practice of the law. Thus when Macedonius revolted on the subject of the Holy Spirit, an assembly was assembled against him at Constantinople by the order of the bishop of Rome; this council rejected the heresiarch and the Church accepted his decision as it had accepted that of the first. She excommunicated Macedonius as she had already excommunicated Arius. She learned from these two councils to say that the Son and the Holy Spirit are of the substance of the Father and that each of them is co-eternal God with the Father. She also accepted these two councils in the same way that the Church of Antioch had previously accepted the Council of the Apostles. Just as the Church of Antioch had no part in the decision of the Apostles, so in these two councils no one discussed. And as what the Apostles had written to the Church of Antioch was considered a decision of the Holy Spirit, so the Church did not doubt that the definition of these two councils was that of the Holy Spirit. Also the Church of Antioch had not accepted the sentiment of Paul and Barnabas nor that of the other brothers, but had brought them to the assembly of the Apostles and awaited the decision of this assembly; when she received it, she was consoled. Thus the Church did not accept the doctrine of Arius nor that of Macedonius, nor those which contradicted them at that time among the Holy Fathers; but she brought the dispute to the holy council and awaited its decision; when she received it, she was consoled and rejoiced. When Nestorius revolted by saying what he said about Christ, the Church rejected his doctrine and brought it, according to its custom, to the holy council, which was assembled at Ephesus by order of the bishop of Rome. The holy council excommunicated him and put an end to his heresy. Holy Church accepted this council and excommunicated Nestorius by rejecting his doctrine, convinced that it had no right to take part in the decision of this council, but that it had the order of the Holy Spirit to do so. submit, as we have already demonstrated. Know well, Nestorian, that you are in error and that you have slipped from the stone on which the Church was built; you are separated from Christ, he no longer dwells in you because you have not accepted the decision of the holy council which the Holy Spirit commanded you to accept as you must accept his own decision. I am very surprised that you follow Nestorius, whom you are not obliged to follow by preferring him to Paul and Barnabas; because the Church did not want to accept what these two lights of men said. But you accepted what Nestorius said and rejected the decision of the council which you are obliged to follow. You took too weak support by trusting in human intelligence and you neglected the assistance of the Holy Spirit. Know again that you have no excuse in this because you received the decisions of the first two councils with confidence and without examination, as the Holy Spirit commands you to do; and you refused this third which the Holy Spirit ordered you to accept with the same submission as the first two councils. You wanted to discuss his judgment and you did not put your trust in the Holy Spirit who assisted him and made him speak. If you allege excuses about this council, know well that Arius and his supporters can easily allege similar excuses against the first council and accuse it of several faults; and Macedonius and his people can also allege similar motives and accuse the second council without fear. As they are not excused and you do not excuse them by accusing these two councils, you must know in the same way that you are not excused before Christ by accusing this third council. When Eutyches and Dioscorus revolted by saying about Christ what they had said about him, the Church rejected their heresy and the Holy Fathers rose up against them. But the Church did not accept their doctrine nor that of those who contradicted them, it had them brought to the judgment of the holy council, according to its custom. The fourth council was then assembled at Chalcedon by the order of the bishop of Rome; he excommunicated them and put an end to their heresy. The Church then accepted the decision of this council, as it had accepted those of the first three councils; she excommunicated Eutyches and Dioscorus and rejected their heresy, knowing well that she had no right to intervene with this council and convinced that her decision was that of the Holy Spirit. You, Jacobite, why have you accepted the three councils with confidence, without discussion, and do you not accept the fourth? You preferred Eutyches and Dioscorus, abandoning the support of the pillar of truth that the Holy Spirit gave you, and you leaned on a broken reed, letting your flesh be cut and your blood spilled, and die so spiritually by your haste to follow those you are not obliged to follow. But this is rather forbidden to you, as you were forbidden to follow the serpent which is the instrument of error. You still do not stop changing the doctrine of one person for that of another, your leaders change your religion and make it like a monster, so that you have well deserved the appellation of Acephales: not having no leader or having several. You have become like a stone displaced from its foundation and which continues to rush, falling to the lowest point of the earth (to the underworld). Thus Eutyches, Dioscorus, Theodosius, Severus, James, and all other heresiarchs have thrown you, each of whom has introduced into your religion the error of his opinion; by contradicting each other, they all contradict the truth. By accusing this holy council, you are not the first among the heretics who accuse the holy councils that they did not want to accept. Indeed. Arius, Macedonius and Nestorius with their supporters blamed with all their might the councils which had excommunicated them; you say less bad things about the Fourth Council than each of them had said against the council which excommunicated it. If you approve of their accusations against previous councils, you must follow them and accept their confession by throwing the yoke of the Holy Spirit from your neck, openly and without concealment. If you condemn their accusation against these holy councils and claim that they are in error by their disobedience to these councils, you must judge in the same way your accusation against the Fourth Council and say that you are in error by your disobedience to these councils. this council. As for the Fifth Council, no one defends the heresy that it excommunicated to discuss with it and treat it as we did with its fellow heretics. When Macarius, Cyrus and Sergius revolted and taught their errors about Christ, the Church refused to accept their opinion and several Fathers rose up against them to discuss them and repel their heresy. But the Church did not absolutely accept their opinion nor that of their adversaries; she brought them to the council, according to her custom. Then the Fifth Council was convened in Constantinople by order of the Bishop of Rome who excommunicated them and put an end to their heresy. Holy

DEMONSTRATION OF THE FAITH

Church welcomed this council as it had received previous councils, abandoning Macarius and his followers and rejecting their heresy. And you, "Monothelite", you received with obedience the first, the second and the third council; you did not see fit to discuss their definitions, as the Holy Spirit forbids you to do; but, having arrived at the Fifth Council, you forgot what the Holy Spirit said, and, like a drunken man, you rose up against your Fathers who deserve your respect, insulting them like a mad dog. The Holy Spirit commands you to obey them, but you wanted to remove their definition and remove the hedge that defended you against Satan; you came out (from the fold of the Church) to be the prey of wolves. You have thus neglected the matter which surely leads you to perdition. If you accuse this holy council, know well that the heretics who were before you preceded you by accusing the councils which had excommunicated them, so that no obstacle prevented them from attributing to these councils everything that Satan had placed on them. in the heart. If you condemn their accusation against these councils, you must likewise condemn your accusation against the Fifth Council and leave your error to enter the right path; but if you approve of their accusation against the holy councils, unmask yourself and follow your friends by believing what all the heresiarchs from the beginning had taught. What results from your accusations, all you heretics, against these councils? Each of you accuses these holy councils of three things, saying: 1° that the council judged badly, with injustice and ignorance; 2° that the council was convoked by the emperor, which is why it should not be accepted; 3° that the previous council had forbidden adding or removing anything to what it had defined; that therefore we must not accept what comes after him. If one of you says, in accusing one of these councils, that he has judged wrongly through ignorance or injustice, the one who says this claims to have the right to discuss the decision of the council or to take part in it; but the Holy Spirit forbids this for himself and for anyone. The pride that swelled him prevented him from submitting to the definition of this council, and he thus deserved spiritual death, as you have heard the law of Moses which does not allow anyone to discuss with the assembly or to consider his opinion better than that of the assembly, under penalty of death. If you say, heretic, of the council which you attack, that it was convoked by the emperor, and that consequently it should not be accepted, for this reason we should not receive any of the previous councils, because all the Councils admitted by all Christians were convened by emperors. It is well known that the First Council of Nicaea was convened by the Emperor Constantine the Great; the second was summoned to

DEMONSTRATION OF THE FAITH

Constantinople by Emperor Theodosius the Great; the third was gathered at Ephesus by Emperor Theodosius the Younger; the fourth was assembled by the emperor Marcian at Chalcedon; the fifth was summoned to Constantinople by Emperor Justinian the Great, and the sixth was summoned by Emperor Constantine, son of Heraclius, to Constantinople. If you reproach, O "Monothelite", the fifth and sixth councils for having been summoned by the emperors, and if you claim that they do not deserve to be accepted because the emperors used force in summoning them and in executing their decrees, you do wrong, because you accept the fourth and all the previous councils which were also summoned by the emperors, as we have said. Any heretic excommunicated by one of these previous councils can say as you do that the emperor who convened this council used his force to excommunicate him and that thus by force this council was convened against him. If you claim to be exempt from the condemnation of these two councils because they were convoked by the emperors, you must necessarily admit that the Jacobites, the Nestorians, Macedonius, Arius and their supporters are exempt from the condemnation of the councils which excommunicated them and who were summoned by the emperors. If you do not believe that they are excepted from the excommunication of these councils because of their convocations by the emperors, neither should you believe yourself to be excepted from the excommunication of the last two councils because they were summoned by the emperors. If you reproach, Jacobite, the fourth council which excommunicated you, for having been summoned by the emperor, saying that it does not deserve to be accepted because the emperor used force for his summons and for the execution of his decrees, you also do wrong, because you accepted the third council and the two previous ones which were all convened by the emperors. You must therefore excuse Arius, Macedonius and Nestorius refusing to accept the decision of the councils which excommunicated them; for everyone can allege this reason like you and say that the emperor used force in convoking this council and in executing his decrees against him. If you allow yourself to thus reject the definition of the fourth council because it was summoned by the emperor, you must necessarily allow all these heretics to reject the definitions of the councils which excommunicated them; if you do not allow them to reject the definitions of the councils which excommunicated them, you must not allow yourself to reject the definition of the fourth council either; otherwise you become unjust and unreasonable. We will say the same thing to you, Nestorian, that we said to the Jacobites and the "Monothelites". You must not reproach the council which excommunicated you for having been summoned by the emperor, nor reject its definition under this pretext; otherwise, you would provide an excuse to Arius and Macedonius who refused to accept the decisions of the councils which condemned them: for they will allege the same reason as you. If you do this, you ruin everything you believe according to these two councils. But this is not a reproach for these councils: it is rather a grace for which the Church must thank Christ who subdued the emperors to thus serve his Fathers and doctors; for every emperor who convened one of these councils thereby became a great benefactor, first by giving hospitality to the Fathers and defending them against the population to allow them to peacefully examine the doctrine, and then by executing the decrees of the council. He had no part in examining the doctrine nor in defining its decrees; he served the Fathers of the council, listened to them and accepted everything they defined regarding the doctrine, without taking part in the discussion. If one of you, heretics who claim to be Christians, reproaches these councils for the assistance of the emperors and their presence among the Fathers, he annuls everything that Christians have, he wants to reduce us to the Old and New Testaments ; we will be able to say like Arius: "The Word is created", or with Macedonius: "The Holy Spirit is created", or with this heretic who makes a breach in the wall of the Church which defended the flock against the hunted ravening wolf ; as a result he corrupts Christian doctrine and makes Christianity a new Judaism. If you say, you, another heretic, when speaking of the council which condemned you, that the previous council had forbidden him to add anything or delete anything to what it had defined and that consequently we must not receive this council which came afterwards, know well that you are saying things which you do not understand and of which you are ignorant of the significance: because the definition of each council is like a particular remedy which the Holy Spirit prepares to keep away from the body of the Church the disease of this heresy condemned by this council. When this council says that it is forbidden for anyone to add or remove from what it has defined, it means that no one is allowed to contradict it and to prepare for the disease of this heresy that he condemned a remedy different from that which he prepared under the inspiration of the Holy Spirit; for the Holy Spirit does not contradict himself. This council cannot tell the Church, if it sees another heresy arise, that it is forbidden for the Fathers who are its doctors to come together to remove this disease as it had removed the disease which agitated the Church from his time. If, by impossibility, this council had acted in this way, it would have left the

Church exposed to all the diseases of heresies of the future and prevented the Fathers from applying proper remedies to it. This would be opposed to the institution of the Holy Spirit who established the councils to replace in the rest of the centuries the college of the Apostles, as Moses had established the assemblies which he had ordered to obey to replace him forever in the function of judge any disputes that arise between judges. If you continue, heretic, by saying that the council accepted by all forbade adding anything or removing anything from its decision, wanting that there would never be another council after it, all councils would have to be annulled, from first to last, because Saint Paul said to the Church: If he himself or an angel from Heaven comes to teach him a doctrine other than that which he taught, let him be accursed. It is therefore permissible for Arius, according to your opinion and according to this quotation, to say to the Council of Nicaea: "I will not accept your doctrine because Saint Paul forbade anyone to teach the Church a doctrine other than the one he himself taught." Macedonius is also permitted to say to the second council: "I will not accept your doctrine because Saint Paul forbade anyone to teach the Church a doctrine other than that which he himself taught, and that the previous council also forbade adding anything to its decision and deleting nothing." If it seems good to you, heretic, you easily reduce us to keeping the books of the Old and the New (Testament), we will be able to say without worry with Arius: "The Son is created", and we will say with impunity with Macedonius: " The Holy Spirit is created", and without fear of being blamed we will confess the doctrine of whomever we please among the heretics, by Judaizing Christianity, as we have already said. But it's quite the opposite. Heretics, you have misunderstood the thoughts of the Fathers; for the holy Church resembles the son of the king, and the Fathers are the doctors to whom the king entrusted the care of preserving his health and keeping away all illness and weakness; but heresies are only illnesses and weaknesses. The doctor to whom his body was entrusted does not commit a fault if, seeing the body of the son of this king seized by an illness, he chases away this illness with appropriate treatment. And if, after that, he comes to say: "It is forbidden for anyone to change the slightest thing in the treatment that I have prescribed", we understand that this doctor only means that it is forbidden for anyone to treat this disease by a treatment different from that which he prescribed himself. This doctor does not say to the doctors who come after him: "If the (body of the) king's son subsequently has another illness, it is not permitted to treat him otherwise"; otherwise he would put the king's child in danger and he would be a traitor and an enemy of the king. Thus each of these holy councils has prepared a remedy specific to the heresy which has arisen in its time, and it has made known to all the world that the remedy which it prescribes is effective and appropriate for the disease of this heresy, and that no one should treat or combat it in any other way than he himself has done. If he forbade the spiritual doctors who would come after him, when another heresy manifests itself in their lives, to prepare another remedy for it and to put an end to the disease, he would be a traitor and enemy of Christ. Would to heaven that a council brought together by the Holy Spirit would never be like this! All of you heretics have misheard the words of the Fathers. Satan, enemy of men, mocks you and, fascinating you, leads you to blaspheme against the Holy Spirit when you censure the decrees of the council which are the decrees of the Holy Spirit himself, as I said . The Apostles, when they pronounced their decision against the heresy which was agitating in their time, declared that "It is the opinion of the Holy Spirit and ours", making known to all the world that their opinion is that of the Holy Spirit; therefore, anyone who blasphemes against the decision of a council blasphemes against the Holy Spirit himself. You said, heretic, of the council which condemned you: It contradicted the council which was before it, if we want to examine its decision carefully; and therefore, as you claim, it is evident that it is not of the Holy Spirit, because the Holy Spirit does not contradict itself. We will answer you, heretic: Your mind is obtuse and you are not enlightened by the Holy Spirit because of your bad faith; This is why you think that this council which condemned you contradicted the previous council. But you must not have a part with this council in its definition if you understand well what the Holy Spirit commanded you through the mouth of Moses chief of the prophets; rather, you must accept the definition of the council under penalty of spiritual death. The Holy Spirit did not allow the assembly of the Apostles to fall in any way into error, since he entrusted them with judging the disputes which would arise on the subject of doctrine, as we have already explained several times: otherwise the Holy Spirit, who required men to obey him, would be the main cause of the error taught to men by this council. Please the Holy Spirit that this is not so. If you allow yourself to censure the decree of the council which condemned you and to criticize its definition, saying that it contradicted the previous council, you must allow for Arius to also censure the definition of the Council of Nicaea which condemned him by saying that his definition is in contradiction with the gospel of the Apostles; we must still allow Macedonius to censure the definition of the second council which condemned him by saying that his word is in contradiction with the definition of the first council. But I don't think you're doing this by claiming to have the right to argue with the council that condemned you. Since you have submitted your objections, all heretics, neither you nor any other, you must not allow yourself to census the holy councils nor oppose in any way their definition; otherwise the Holy Spirit would have needlessly ordered, through the mouth of Moses, chief of the prophets, to put to death anyone who does not accept the definition of the council: otherwise, everyone could accuse the council if this council pronounces judgment against him; and he could refuse to accept his decision for this false accusation and save himself from the penalty of spiritual death; but the Holy Spirit left no one this freedom; moreover, he clearly pronounced the death penalty against anyone who did not submit to the definition of the council, and this for anyone whoever they may be, without exception; he leaves no one with a pretext to avoid death by accusing this council or by acting in any other way. Know well, all you heretics, that you all fall under this threat: whoever disobeys these holy councils, Christ condemns him to death, and he strips you of the Holy Spirit who dwelt in your hearts. See who should live there. Know this well, all you who are rebels against the Holy Spirit: whoever among you does not claim to be knowledgeable, we have enlightened him on the path of truth, and he will have no excuse by rejecting the holy councils to which he already knows he is bound to submit; nothing can keep him from the kingdom of God or driven from the nuptial feast of Christ if he follows these holy councils; and he who claims to be learned is like the priests of the Jews and the Pharisees who prevented the Jews from hearing the teaching of the Holy Spirit and gave them the dregs of their obscure intelligence to make them drunk, so that they misunderstood the Christ announced by Holy Scripture and, seduced by them, they crucified him. Thus you have deceived these unfortunate people by preventing them from obeying the Holy Spirit who made these holy councils speak; you offered them the dirt of your obscure intelligence and what you study in the blindness of your hearts; you have made them blaspheme against the Holy Spirit. You are thus lost and you have lost the others, you have chained those who follow you to the bottom of hell; but the devil chains you all, he keeps you as companions in the fire of hell prepared for him and for his angels, you are his consolation and his joy there. Would any of you pretend to put himself on one side and put the council on the other, and say: "men, do not believe this council, but believe me, for I know more than he, I am more recommendable than him? when did you deserve to have this wisdom or rather this blindness more than all men? When then did you become the most clear-sighted of all men in their interests, or rather the greatest deceiver? It would have been necessary for the Holy Spirit to have made you known to men a long time ago, if you are really what you think you are, so that they could be fixed on your personality; he would have had to characterize you as he had characterized this council; he would have had to give the signs of cognoscibility in Holy Scripture as he had done for this council; Moreover, he would have had to force men to follow you as he had forced them to follow this council. But I am not surprised by this, blind person who knows neither what you say nor what you reason, as Saint Paul speaks; you are so ignorant and so enveloped by the darkness of error, that you no longer feel your state. I am rather surprised to see these unfortunate people abandon obedience to these holy councils according to the order of the Holy Spirit and let themselves be led by you like the blind man of whom Our Lord speaks in the Gospel: "A blind leads another blind and both fall into the same pit." And as St. Paul says: "They have taken many false teachers like you because of the itching of their ears." (II Tim, IV, 3.) But we, Orthodox and children of holy Church, give glory and thanksgiving to Christ, our God, who has granted us good will and obedience to the holy councils that the Holy Spirit spoke. We are in his house and in the fold of his flocks. By his protection, we are saved from Satan who, like a devouring wolf, prowls around our souls to surprise anyone who ventures to leave the Church and make him his prey. We implore our Lord and our God Jesus Christ to establish us forever on the rock of his holy Church and to make us drink the liquor of his sweet doctrine. We will thus be intoxicated with his love which fills our souls and our hearts with joy and happiness by leading us to obey him by observing his commandments, to live eternally and inherit his heavenly kingdom prepared for all that has been built on the foundation of Saint Peter by the Holy Spirit. Holy Spirit, make us know Christ, the eternal Son of God, who became incarnate of the Virgin Mary through the Holy Spirit for our salvation. To Him be the glory, the power, the majesty and the worship, with the Father and the Holy Spirit, now and always, for ever and ever. So be it.

The Scriptorium Project is the work of a small group of lay people of various apostolic churches who are interested in the preservation, transmission, and translation of the works of the early and medieval church. Our efforts are to make the works of the church fathers accessible to anyone who might have an interest in Christian antiquities and the theological, philosophical, and moral writings that have become the bedrock of Western Civilization.

To-date, our releases have pulled from the Greek, Syriac, Georgian, Latin, Celtic, Ethiopian, and Coptic traditions of Christianity, and have been pulled from sundry local traditions and languages.

www.ingramcontent.com/pod-product-compliance
Lightning Source LLC
LaVergne TN
LVHW061043070526
838201LV00073B/5163